Hearing Horses Chasing Zebras

A LOGICAL LOOK AT THE BEGINNING

James Budds

WESTBOW
PRESS®
A DIVISION OF THOMAS NELSON
& ZONDERVAN

Scripture quotations are from The Holy Bible, English Standard Version® (ESV®), copyright © 2001 by Crossway, a publishing ministry of Good News Publishers. Used by permission. All rights reserved.

This book is a work of non-fiction. Unless otherwise noted, the author and the publisher make no explicit guarantees as to the accuracy of the information contained in this book and in some cases, names of people and places have been altered to protect their privacy.

WestBow Press books may be ordered through booksellers or by contacting:

WestBow Press
A Division of Thomas Nelson & Zondervan
1663 Liberty Drive
Bloomington, IN 47403
www.westbowpress.com
1 (866) 928-1240

Because of the dynamic nature of the Internet, any web addresses or links contained in this book may have changed since publication and may no longer be valid. The views expressed in this work are solely those of the author and do not necessarily reflect the views of the publisher, and the publisher hereby disclaims any responsibility for them.

Any people depicted in stock imagery provided by Thinkstock are models, and such images are being used for illustrative purposes only. Certain stock imagery © Thinkstock.

ISBN: 978-1-5127-4807-9 (sc)
ISBN: 978-1-5127-4808-6 (e)

Library of Congress Control Number: 2016910430

Print information available on the last page.

WestBow Press rev. date: 06/23/2016

Contents

Acknowledgments

I would like to thank my wife, Patti, for her encouragement, patience, and understanding during the time it took to bring this book together. Thank you to my boys, Sean and Alex, even if you don't know it, you both were a big part of this process. I would also like to thank Duwayne and Shannon for your comments and critics to help me make this book the best I could. Also thank you to Jennifer for your not-so-subtle prods.

Introduction

This book is meant to be a logical exploration of creation versus evolution. This book is not intended to be a text book. There will be no sixteen-letter words. And while there will be a few references to research and other people's ideas, the premise of this book is to stop and think through the beliefs secular scientists and Creationists hold. To simplify matters I will use the term "evolutionists" to represent the secular scientific community in general. This includes the areas of biology, physics, astronomy, and any other scientific discipline interested in the beginning of things.

This is not the meat and potatoes of the arguments. This book is designed to be the broth the meat and potatoes were cooked in. All the "flavor" is there but I hope I have made it easier to digest. During the course of this journey we will try to determine simply which makes the most sense.

So who is this book written for? There are three main groups of people I hope will give a thorough read to the thoughts presented. The first are those people who doubt creation and view it as an illogical way to make some ancient myth more believable. The second are those who are unsure what they believe and what they should believe. They may not have fully considered how the beginning of the universe and life occurred, but they have questions that they would like answers to. The third group are Christians who may struggle to answer questions presented by atheists or non-believers when the subject of the origins of life are brought up. Some may not feel prepared to discuss logical concepts that will help them explain their belief in a Creator, but would like to.

For too long those who believe in a creator have been seen as ignorant, uneducated, illogical, and foolish. My hope is that this book will show there is logic to the idea of a Creator. When one looks at both evolution and creationism through the same lens, that of logic, one view will stand out as making the most sense.

Chapter One

If you are walking the streets of eighteenth-century London and hear hoof beats, you should look for a horse, not a zebra.

In the course of this book we will be looking at the view points of evolution and creation. While we look at these two differing ideas we will be looking through the lens of logic, focused by Occam's razor. Occam's razor is an idea that states the simplest explanation that completely answers a question is the correct one. There are two points to this idea that I believe are crucial.

The first characteristic of this principle is simplicity. It is easy to come up with several answers to a question. If one is a good storyteller, he or she can weave quite a tale going through several points before reaching the destination. This works well for novelists and scriptwriters, but it does little to help the scientist or philosopher. Let's look at an exaggerated version of this as an example.

A child asks the question, "What is the color green?" Some answers that could be given include "green is the combination of blue and yellow" or "green is what happens when an object absorbs all the colored light on the spectrum other than green light. This green light is reflected back, and that is why we see something as green."

Another, more interesting answer could be that a comet was circling through the galaxy and passed through a nebula, picking up a colored dust. This comet eventually made its way to Earth impacting the planet and spreading this colored dust throughout the atmosphere. Everything the dust stuck to is now the color we know as green. All three of these examples give us an answer to what is the color green?

The first explanation is the simplest. However, it does not fully answer the question as a logical follow-up question would be, "Where do blue and yellow come from?" This brings us to the second point when dealing with Occam's razor. The correct answer needs to be the simplest answer, but it has to be the simplest answer that completely answers the question. In this example of the color green, the second explanation is more complicated than the first but more completely answers the question. This answer is also much simpler than the third explanation, which does not completely answer the question to begin with. We will look more closely at these explanations later.

I was in a high school science class when I first heard of Occam's razor. When this was presented to the class, I remember the example being of eighteenth-century London. The teacher stated if you are walking the streets of eighteenth-century London and hear hoof beats, you should look for a horse, not a zebra. How does this give us an example of Occam's razor? Doesn't this just seem like a simple given? This idea seems pretty basic, almost not even worth bringing up. Unfortunately, in today's climate, it seems that unless something is complicated and hard to understand, many people refuse to believe it or give it any scientific credibility.

Before we jump into the more in-depth subjects we wish to examine in later chapters, let us practice looking at ideas and situations logically. To do this, we will look more closely at the two examples we have so far. We will look first at the horse and zebra.

The first thing we want to consider is whether both explanations, in this case if the hoof beats are from a horse or a zebra, are possible. In order to determine this, we need to look at the most probable manner in which the explanation could have come about. We will start with the horse.

By the eighteenth century, horses were prominent in London. Horses were used to pull carriages, and they were also used for riding. When walking through a large, busy city such as London, it would be quite unusual *not* to see a horse. Thus hearing hoof beats on cobblestone would be common and would almost certainly originate from a horse. Given this our horse option is possible.

So what about the zebra? It is entirely plausible that by the eighteenth century, London could have had a zoo. It is not a stretch to think a zebra may have been captured in its native Africa and transported to this zoo in London. At some point, this zebra could have escaped its enclosure at the zoo. Upon escaping its enclosure, the zebra would have then traveled through-out the zoo undetected, managing to escape the zoo entirely. This zebra - transported from Africa to reside in the London zoo from which it escaped at least two enclosures - is now wandering the streets of London. As it meanders the streets of London, it comes close enough to your location that you can hear it on the cobblestone street nearby. Given this, the zebra option is also possible.

If both of these are possible we apply Occam's razor. Clearly, the horse answer is the simplest, but does it completely answer the question of which animal is making the noise I am hearing? I believe it does; the horse making the sound is the logical answer given the parameters of Occam's razor.

Let us now move on to our explanations of the color green.

We have already seen that simply stating green is the combination of the colors blue and yellow - though possible and on the surface accurate - is an incomplete answer. "What is blue?" and "what is yellow?" become follow-up questions that require answers. At the heart of the question about the color green is a question about the nature of all colors. Deflecting this question does not answer the base question, which makes this an incomplete and unacceptable answer.

Let us skip ahead for a moment to our space-traveling comet. This answer seems possible on the surface. However, when we start looking at whether it fully answers the question, we run into problems with its possibility. One question would be about where does the dust goes when green things change color, such as leaves and grass in the fall. If this color green is a result of adhered dust, wouldn't we eventually run out of green? Taking this line of reasoning even further, one could ask, if a comet impacted the earth somewhere, why is there not a greater concentration of green things in that area? Also, if green is a result of dust, how did things become green that are exclusively under water? Just as with the simple answer of green as the result of combining blue and yellow, comet dust does not answer this question for other colors. Are all colors a result of interstellar dust? If not, where did other colors come from and why is green different?

As you can see, there are too many questions that are unanswered to allow our comet theory to be possible. And if by some stretch someone thought this may be possible, this theory certainly is not simple.

But what about light absorbed and reflected? A simple prism shows us light is made of many different colors, including green. We know plants absorb light to produce nutrients for themselves. We know light can be reflected off various things such as water, mirrors, and metal. While we know things other than plants are green, there is no leap between plants and other objects being able to absorb some light and reflect others.

This theory of absorbing and reflecting light appears possible and fully answers the question of what is green. Other questions may arise about why some objects do not absorb green light or why light is made up of different colors, but these are ancillary questions. These do not speak to the root of the original question as the combination of colors did in our first theory.

Moving forward we will be using the foundation laid in this chapter to look at the beginnings of the universe, early life, and life as we know it today. We will use the principle of Occam's razor to examine the most logical reasons behind these beginnings. In the end, the most logical theory - the one that makes the most sense - is the one we should hold on to.

Chapter Two

In the beginning, God created the heavens and the earth.

-Genesis 1:1

Our whole universe was in a hot dense state, Then nearly fourteen billion years ago expansion started... It all started with the big bang!

-Barenaked Ladies

The predominant theory about the birth of the universe today is the big bang theory. Though not everyone subscribes to the big bang theory, the vast majority of evolutionary scientists and many creationists have now adopted this theory. The difference is the view of the ultimate origin of the big bang.

For those unfamiliar with the big bang theory, the theory basically states at one time in the distant past (or relatively recent past, depending on your particular bias), everything needed for everything currently in existence was condensed in an unimaginably dense, hot, concentrated ball of material that reached its breaking point and flung all this material in every direction. From this material all that we know came to be. The difference between evolutionists and creationists on this subject is whether this explosive beginning started either by happenstance or by a creator putting a plan into action.

Up until the last few decades, most scientists viewed the universe as static and eternal. With an eternal universe, a creator was more than unnecessary - a creator would have been impossible. The idea of a universe in motion, spreading away from a center point came from Einstein's theory of relativity. Einstein's formulas showed an expanding universe contradicting previous thoughts that assumed the universe to be static.

A static universe does not mean there is no movement. Obviously things in the universe move. It had been suspected since the third century BC the earth not only rotated but revolved around the sun as well. When viewing the universe as being in a static state, scientists believed each galaxy, solar system, and other celestial bodies had been in the same basic place forever. In a modern scientific age, this eternal universe was thought to push a created universe into the same category as Greek and Roman mythologies with their stories of gods, monsters, and heroes.

So who cares if the universe is moving? How does a universe in motion affect its eternality? If objects are steadily moving away from one point and spreading out, it stands to reason at one time those objects were closer together than they are now. Working backwards, one gets the hot, dense, concentrated ball of stuff said to be present just prior to the big bang. If the universe can be traced back to a starting point it cannot be eternal.

If one accepts this premise, then the question becomes what happened before the big bang and where did the material for the big bang come from? A secularist scientist would say our technology has yet to reach the level of sophistication necessary to answer this question. They would tell you they know without a doubt there is a scientific answer and one day we will be able to see past the ultra-dense universe and know where it came from. They would say that though they cannot do that now, give them time and they will come up with the answer that most certainly does not involve a creator. Scientists would say the big bang proves there is no creator since there is an explanation as to how the universe got its start without the intervention of an outside being or source.

On the other hand, a creationist would say the universe starting from a single point in time sounds a lot like the creation story in Genesis. A creationist would argue God started the big bang and the material involved came from the creative power of God. For the creationist a look past the moment of the bang makes little difference as there would be nothing there.

Scientists believe throwing in a creator to fill in the gap is merely a cop-out explanation. This may be true, but at this point creationists have a cop-out and evolutionists have a "wait and see."

Chapter Three

And God made the two great lights—the greater light to rule the day and the lesser light to rule the night—and the stars.

-Genesis 1:16

We find, therefore, under this orderly arrangement, a wonderful symmetry in the universe, and a definite relation of harmony in the motion and magnitude of the orbs, of a kind that is not possible to obtain in any other way.

-Johannes Kepler

Now that the universe has been birthed, a look at the structure and organization of the cosmos is in order. When exploring a topic such as this it can be quite easy to bury ourselves in details and never be able to come back up for air. While I have every intent to be as thorough as necessary, the purpose of this book is to step back a bit and look at the big picture of life. Some details are necessary and will be presented. But again, this is not a text book on astrophysics.

Having said that, let us start near home - with our solar system - and branch out from there. One thing that is evident no matter which perspective you look through is that our solar system operates on an incredibly precise mechanism. From the distance of the planets from each other and the sun, to the consistency and predictability of near circular orbits, our solar system is an example of fine-tuned machinery.

The distance of the earth from the sun is a major factor in being able to maintain temperatures necessary for life as we know it. If the earth was a little closer or farther from the sun, life would not be sustainable. Closer would cause all of the water on Earth to evaporate. Any farther away would create a perpetual ice age not allowing for liquid water.

Since the distance from the sun is key in maintaining an environment suitable to life it is important Earth maintain a consistent distance from the sun. This requires a near circular orbit. In order to maintain this, the other planets in the solar system must cooperate not be able to pull Earth from this all important orbit shape. This can either be achieved by not having planets big enough to pull a life filled planet out of orbit or by having those planets maintain orbital patterns which do not interfere with Earth's orbit. Excluding large planets raises other problems. Large gas giant planets in the solar system protect the Earth from comets. The sizeable gravitational influence of these gas giants allow only a few comets to enter the interior of the solar system.

Distance and consistency around the sun are key components for life on this planet. But will any sun do? Pick a bright spot in the sky and assume it will work for life? Unfortunately, this is not the case. The size of the sun, the temperature, stability, and even the age of the star is vital to sustaining life such as we have on Earth.

And what of the size of the Earth? Would any planet a certain distance from a star work? Again the answer is no. Earth, with its liquid core, plated crust, and ideal size appears to be custom made for life. The core and size of Earth determine the level of gravity exerted on everything dwelling on the surface. Too much gravity and the physical structure of nearly everything we know would be vastly different. Too little gravity and not only would those things on the surface not permanently attached float off but our atmosphere would as well. All of these aspects intertwine like gears in a fine watch for life as we know it to exist in the only place we know it does.

Astronomers are finding more and more planets orbiting suns in other solar systems. Internet news pages often run stories about the latest planetary find - some touting headlines asking if the newly discovered planet is the next Earth. Of the nearly one thousand planets discovered circling other suns none meet the basic requirements of being around a properly sized sun, being the proper size, and orbiting in the habitable zone of that star.

This says nothing of the large protective planets, suitable orbits, and a moon for added protection and tidal stabilization. As you can see, finding the right structural components of a solar system capable of bearing life is quite some feat. But could all of the components come together in a natural unassisted way? Evolutionists will, in fact, acknowledge the difficulty of the exact components coming together perfectly in one try.

In order to compensate for this difficulty, evolutionists propose there is not one universe that met these astronomical variables but several - maybe millions of universes. In some of these universes the big bang hasn't/won't happen. In others life evolved in radically different ways. And if you are a fan of science fiction some universes are close to ours, just off a little. If there is a one in millions chance life evolved as it has on Earth, then there must be millions of universes.

This argument is comparable to the following scenario. A person, call her Gabby, one day decides she is going to run a 5K. She hasn't really run before but is in good shape and 5K isn't that far. The problem is she doesn't know how far 5K is and has no way of measuring it. To solve this problem, she makes hundreds of herself and they just set out running, all of them stopping at different points. Surely one of them will have run exactly five kilometers.

Where did all the additional Gabby's come from? No one really knows and Gabby isn't talking. This is a major problem evolutionists have to answer with the multi universe theory. Evolution has yet to provide a reasonable beginning to the universe we are all aware of - let alone millions of other universes.

These examples of the finely tuned universe are far from exhaustive. If we wanted to dig even further we could look at the strength of gravity, tilt of the Earth, position of the solar system in the galaxy, distance of the galaxies from each other, makeup of the Earth's atmosphere, and the gaseous mix of our sun. And these are just to name a few.

Chapter Four

And God said, "Let the earth bring forth living creatures according to their kinds— livestock and creeping things and beasts of the earth according to their kinds." And it was so.

-Genesis 1:24

Evolution is the fundamental idea in all of life science – in all of biology.

-Bill Nye

So now, whether by chance or by choice, there is an ideally sized fledgling Earth in the optimum setting to sustain life as we currently know it. The next obvious question that needs to be answered is how life began on this planet. Did life begin in its most rudimentary form or as individual species, primarily as-is?

Before we can really answer this question, we should have a brief discussion of "simple" life. We will begin with single celled organisms, what they are comprised of, how they function, and move up from there. We will look at the possibility of advanced organisms growing from these seemingly simple pieces of life.

Basic life is formed from proteins. Proteins are formed from amino acids. There are twenty different amino acids which form the basis for proteins in all life; there are hundreds of identified amino acids found in nature[1]. Through experimentation scientists have been able to recreate conditions which they feel were present on an infant Earth which could have led to the beginnings of life.

Some of these experiments include simulating a comet strike on a primordial Earth, and a lightning strike through a potential early atmosphere. Another theory suggests lava vents in the ocean were prime locations for the basic elements of life as we know it to develop. Through these experiments, scientists have been able to create amino acids, but only a few at a time. It is important to have perspective on what this handful of amino acids amounts to. Proteins contain anywhere from 39 to 8,200 amino acids. This is not the number of amino acids in a single cell, or a single cell organism, but a single protein. And all these amino acids have to be in the right order or the protein is not functional.

In the average cell, proteins make up ten to twenty-five percent of the cell's weight. Much of the rest of the weight is accounted for by water. This means there are an almost innumerable number of amino acids in any given cell.

Now whether through lightning strikes, comet impacts, lava vents, or some other means, we have at least one pool of amino acids. There are now enough of these very basic components to create a protein. Just the right amino acids have to come together in just the right way to create a viable protein. This then has to happen dozens upon dozens of times to create the right proteins to make, say a cell membrane. The cell membrane is needed to keep all of the insides, inside.

A closer look at the cell membrane shows a double line of molecules called lipids. These lipids are organized to keep the part of them that dislikes water pointed inward. This maintains a barrier which things cannot get through. But cells need things from the outside world and sometimes they need to get rid of things from the inside. In order to do this the membrane needs channels. These are called protein channels. Spread throughout the membrane are these channels, specifically designed to allow certain things in or out of the cell but to not respond to anything else. Think of it as the child's shape sorting toy. If you try and put the star shaped block in the star shaped hole you get a star shaped block on the inside of the box. If you try and put the square block through the star shaped hole, you will not have a square block inside the box.

The cell membrane is just one aspect of a cell. In fact, one must not make the mistake of thinking because a cell is small it is simple. In fact, the average cell as several components[2]:

- Nucleus
- Mitochondria
- Chloroplasts (plant cells)
- Ribosomes
- Endoplasmic reticulum (both smooth and rough)
- Golgi body
- Vesicles
- Tubules and filaments

This is not an exhaustive list and depending on the type of cell one could also find cilia and flagellum for movement.

We hear of all these amazing things science is able to do with cells these days in making one type of cell into a different type of cell, or adding information to cells to treat different ailments. And we might think, if science can make new cells it can't be that difficult. One thing to remember though is that science is not creating new cells from nothing.

I bought an old truck from a friend of mine once. It used to be a diesel engine farm truck; it still had part of the cattle guard on the front of it. When it was no longer being used on the farm, someone decided to make the truck into a regular gasoline powered truck. In order to do this, they had to remove the old engine and replace it with a new one out of a different vehicle. The truck now ran different, and did something different than before. But no one created a new truck out of nothing. They borrowed from something that already existed. As amazing as science's use of cells is, they are simply using material they have found. We still can't make a cell from nothing, they are simply too complicated.

Much like the human body as a whole, cells have various systems that must work together to keep the cell alive and viable until the point it reproduces itself. We'll get back to that in just a minute. In order to look in-depth at how a cell functions I would have to break my sixteen letter rule. To keep things as simple as possible I'll just say the above cell components work as a brain, protein factories, energy producers, and waste management. Depending on the type of cell there will be other components to allow each cell to do its individual job or work together for a bigger job.

One question to consider is, in the beginning when cells first formed, was there one cell or multiple cells that came together at the same time? Either answer presents its own set of problems. Let us start with the second answer first. Having several cells develop at the same time would require a very large, relatively speaking, pool of amino acids to come together just right to make the right proteins to come together in just the right way several times to create a pool of cells. Assuming all this happened it is not hard to see these cells would most likely be very similar given the same environmental conditions.

Or would they? Maybe the proteins came together differently. Maybe there were several different kinds of cells that developed at the same time in the same place with the same materials.

That adds another layer of complexity to this scenario. Another question would be if they all survived, or a couple, or one?

Given the number of things needed to come together in just the right way it is easy to imagine the one developed cell scenario. But did it survive long enough by itself to reproduce? Did it fail and the mix had to start over again? How many restarts of randomly selected bases had to occur for that first cell to be viable enough to reproduce and become two cells?

Like humans and babies, if a cell wants to pass along its genetic code it has to reproduce. This generally means first copying the cell's DNA - the blueprint for everything in the cell - separating the copies and then having the cell pinch off. This effectively creates two identical cells. Was this the first method early cells tried for reproduction? Were there other attempts that did not work? How many reproduction strategies had to be enlisted across how many cells to get this accomplished? We are back to the same question of how many initial cells and how many times did a haphazard process have to play out in order to sustain basic early life. I mean, if life started with a single cell that was lucky enough to win the chance lottery to build itself effectively enough to live, to figure out reproduction, and to accomplish it, that would be amazing! Almost miraculous. On the other hand, if numerous restarts had to happen and did, that is almost just as amazing.

What about the material for these restarts? Was all the basic material formed at one time via lightening or meteor strike? Did this event have to happen several times for additional restarts? Counting on the same random event to produce the same result certainly seems like a long shot.

The premise of evolution is change through successful mutations, making the organism better suited for its environment. This means somewhere along the line of single celled life and reproduction, something had to go wrong. Mutations generally happen when an error occurs in the copying of a cell's DNA - when the cell divides this creates one mutated cell. How many unsuccessful mutations were there before a beneficial one? How many standard cell divisions occurred before the first mutation? At what point did the division between plant and animal cells occur? Did the cells change the environment? Did the environment change the cells? Both?

These are questions there are not answers for, at least not yet. Suffice it to say, an evolutionary understanding of the start of cellular life is laden with either a great deal of luck and good fortune or an almost unimaginable number of false starts and second chances.

Chapter Five

And God said, "Let the earth sprout vegetation, plants yielding seed, and fruit trees bearing fruit in which is their seed, each according to its kind, on the earth. And it was so. The earth brought forth vegetation, plants yielding seed according to their own kinds, and trees bearing fruit in which is their seed, each according to its kind. And God saw that it was good.

-Genesis 1:11-12

There's almost no food that isn't genetically modified. Genetic modification is the basis of all evolution. Things change because our planet is subjected to a lot of radiation, which causes DNA damage, which gets repaired, but results in mutations, which create a ready mixture of plants that people can choose from to improve agriculture.

-Nina Fedoroff

At this time, I believe it would be wise to take a brief detour in our conversation and discuss a couple of different types of evolution. Evolution is a broader term which contains both micro-evolution and macro-evolution.

There is no argument amongst either the secular or creation science camps regarding micro-evolution. Micro-evolution is simply a characteristic of a species becoming more prominent over another. There tend to be more white rabbits in snowy climates than in areas closer to the equator.

For the rest of our discussion when we talk about evolution I will be speaking of macro-evolution which is the major change bridging an old species with a new one. Creationists would deny micro-evolution leads to macro-evolution.

Now that we have clarified some terms let us continue on with the conversation. As mentioned in the previous chapter, somewhere along the potential path of evolution, the single living cells began to differentiate between animal cells and plant cells. The two primary characteristics differentiating animal and plant cells are the pant cells' addition of a wall and chloroplasts. These vague categories of cells are the basis for numerous species of life. Looking on the surface of multi-celled organisms which fall into the plant and animal categories, we see some other basic differences. Plants are generally stationary while animals are generally mobile. Plants are usually green or have some aspect which is green. Animals tend to be more diverse in color. There are exceptions to these broad observations but it helps to note the differences, even the obvious ones, as we move forward in our discussion.

Somewhere along the line of our single celled living organism multiplying itself, something happened. A mistake happened. The code that tells the cell everything it needs to know about itself changed. This new cell now acts differently and potentially looks different. How big this change may have been will be discussed in a later chapter.

Whether a large or small change this new life has begun a journey down two separate paths. One path goes towards the animals that exist now; another path leads to the plants we know now. Where exactly this split may have occurred no one can say.

In this chapter we will be focusing on the path of plants. One aspect of evolution often talked about is survival of the fittest. According to survival of the fittest, the organism best suited to survive, or better yet to thrive in its environment, will pass along those traits to future generations.

We can see survival of the fittest (not to mention micro-evolution) on a smaller scale by the way scientists and farmers have manipulated various types of plants. For instance, many vegetables are cross-bred to bring out certain traits they wish to emphasize. We will see this in aspects of the animal kingdom as well once we get there.

One plant often manipulated is the tomato. Tomatoes today are often larger, have thicker skins, spoil more slowly, and bruise less easily. This is to allow them to be shipped long distances and still look pretty once they hit the store shelves - so consumers will want to buy them. One unintended drawback to these advantages may be a decrease in the quality of the flavor of these tomatoes.

Creative scientists have come up with new twists on the old boring fruits many of us remember. Now there are such things as tangelos and grapples and pluerry and peacharine and pluot and...? So here is evidence of new species being created by evolution right? Maybe, or maybe not, but we'll discuss further shortly. Again the idea here is to take aspects of something that is desirable, and mix it with something else that is desirable and end up with something completely desirable.

The idea is, this happens spontaneously in nature as well. So if I put a cherry tree next to a plum tree I'll end up with a plueery tree in the middle? What about a peach tree next to a nectarine tree? Apple tree next to a grape vine? What if I grow a grape vine up an apple tree? These are changes we just don't see in nature. The combining of various fruits or vegetables requires a fair amount of knowledge and manipulation of the plants' DNA.

But what about our friend the tomato from a few paragraphs ago? What if we find a tomato plant that seems to have above average sized tomatoes and cross-breed it with another plant that has large tomatoes. Does that lend itself to bigger tomatoes in the next generation? Most likely, yes. But how big can you get a tomato? Apparently a bit over eight pounds[3]. That is the world record for the heaviest tomato. Why not a tomato the size of a watermelon, a watermato? Because tomato DNA has boundaries built into it. Without manipulating the DNA directly, you can push to the upper limits more often but not exceed them.

An intelligent plant expert trying to specifically increase one aspect of the plant, in this case its size, can only go so far - why would a haphazard trial and error come up with differing results? It is true very smart people have figured out how to manipulate the DNA of certain plants to create new combinations. But they are taking fruits and making fruits. They are not taking fruits and making eggs. We can make sweeter corn and juicier oranges buy combining sweeter and juicier plants, and this may happen spontaneously in nature, but this does not in anyway change the fundamentals of the orange or corn.

Aside from allowing specific plants to survive in specific areas, one would be hard pressed to point toward survival of the fittest to explain the survival of entire species in an area. It is true you won't find many palm trees in Alaska but is that because through evolution, a common ancestor split towards two species, one a pine tree and one a palm? Somewhere along the line did the palm cousin decide it just couldn't make it in snow? Do all trees have to be related to a single ancestor? Again we have to glance back at the previous chapter on single celled organisms and how they would have changed and evolved.

Continuing with survival of the fittest scientists backing this theory often use it to explain diversity. Looking at the world of plants, does survival of the fittest work to create diversity or is this a contradiction? We don't have to look too closely to see this is actually a contradiction. If survival of the fittest worked as we expected it to, at a certain point in evolution all plants in a given area should look exactly the same. For instance, why in one natural forest can you find pine trees, oaks, maples, elms, and ash trees? Is it better in the forests of the Appalachian Mountains to have needle leaves or broad maple leaves? What about pine cones versus acorns or helicopter seed pods? These trees are all quite different yet thrive equally in the same environment. Survival of the fittest would tell us one of these trees or maybe even a combined species would survive the best, and thus be the lone type of tree. We simply do not see this. While humans have found various uses for the various types of trees there does not appear to be any reason in nature to have so many different species. Especially when many of the species occupy the same environments.

Why so many kinds of nut trees? I enjoy the various types of nuts but why does nature, purely looking at survival, need almonds and pecans and hazel nuts? Again we would expect one type of tree that produces one type of nut. Or for efficiency's sake, one tree that produces all kinds of nuts!

Just for the sake of conversation, I want to ask another question. People have been cutting down trees for millennia. This along with the natural felling of trees from wind and lightning one would think trees would have at least started to evolve a more metallic or maybe a petrified bark to allow them to survive longer.

Moving away from trees for minute, let us look now at other plants. The number of plant species in the world is head spinning. When you consider grasses, flowers, grains, bushes, and the trees we've already spoken of. We just looked at the variety of trees as an example of the problem with creating variations in types of trees. We could have easily looked at the various types of any of the above mentioned plant types. And that list is far from exhaustive. If we assume all plants have a common ancestor due to the original single celled organism, something needs to account for this variety. The mutating of different characteristics which make a plant more successful appears to be much more of a zebra than the horse.

Chapter Six

---

*And God said, "Let the waters swarm
with swarms of living creatures, and
let birds fly above the earth across
the expanse of the heavens." So God
created the great sea creatures and
every living creature that moves, with
which the waters swarm, according
to their kinds, and every winged bird
according to its kind. And God saw
that it was good. And God blessed
them, saying, "Be fruitful and
multiply and fill the waters in the
seas, and let birds multiply on the*

earth." And there was evening and there was morning, the fifth day.

And God said, "Let the earth bring forth living creatures according to their kinds—livestock and creeping things and beasts of the earth according to their kinds." And it was so. And God made the beasts of the earth according to their kinds and the livestock according to their kinds, and everything that creeps on the ground according to its kind. And God saw that it was good.

-Genesis 1:20-25

Animals come from nature. They were not designed. All my inspiration comes from nature, whether it's an animal or the layout of bark or of a leaf. Sometimes my patterns are very bold, and you can barely see where they come from, but all the textures and all the prints come out of nature.

-Diane von Furstenberg

If slow mutation gave rise to the vast variety of plant species, the same must be true of animals as well. As discussed before, a separation must have taken place in the reproduction of that single, successful cell in order to create such extremely different types of living organisms as plants and animals. However, once the animal string was established incredible mutations would have to have taken place to account for the level of variety we see today.

For those who put humans in the category of animals, be assured we will discuss humans in the next chapter. For now, we will focus on what would more traditionally be considered wild animals. Or now, domesticated animals such as livestock and pets.

Let us start at the beginning - where the library of animal species received its start. At some point in the evolution of life, the single celled organism mutated with predominately animal characteristics. These would be cells without cell walls or chloroplasts for energy. Animal cells must be the frontrunner to plant cells. It would make no sense for plant cells, containing additional characteristics, to have come first, then lose those characteristics to become animal cells, but continue to flourish. Apparently the addition of cell walls and chloroplasts allowed for the start of a completely new life form without detracting from the success of its predecessor - the animal cell.

The prevailing theory for where this happened is in a body of water. Many evolutionists believe animal life began in an aquatic environment then moved onto land. Much of this theory may come from the animal which currently exists known as the walking fish. There are various species of these walking fish, from aggressive razor tooth snakeheads to cute hoppy Pacific leaping blennies.

If animals did in fact start in the water, having a transitional creature such as a walking fish makes perfect sense. One major problem with this theory is what prompted water based life to have to go land based to survive? There is much more water on the planet than land. Was there a food shortage? How did the animals thriving in the water survive?

In evolutionary theory change is accidental but helpful. The idea is if the change, the mutation, the mistake is not helpful it will go away. If a water creature developed a mutation which was more beneficial on land, how would it know? What would prompt this creature to test this adaptation? Would this animal have the reasoning capacity to figure out there is an environment other than water and it could do quite well in this environment?

What was this specific adaptation? Did it allow the creature to live full time on land, or like the walking fish, did it have to return to the water? Did this creature survive more successfully on aquatic food or land based food? Again we can't know what happened to eventually push this creature, or its descendants, on land for good.

Another potential scenario could be life starting in water, moving entirely on land, then having some life return to the water. This would account for both land and water creatures. This idea does raise several other questions, however. If we take from the previous conversation of a water creature moving to land, we have to assume either all other water creatures were no longer able to survive for some reason or they all mutated to adapt to the land. Or maybe a little bit of both.

From here it is not too hard to have life move back into the water. Water is an essential ingredient in life as we know it. There is little reason to believe this would not have always, or nearly always, been the case. If an amphibious creature developed and found it had more success in the water with food, protection, and room you could see how they may develop further compensations to remain there. Also, it is much easier to fall into water than it is to pull yourself up onto land.

This would mean, however, water based life would have had to evolve two separate times. This seems to be pushing the boundaries of logical evolution. But there is a solution to this double evolution. What if we skip the idea animal life first developed in water? What if we start with animals on land that evolved to survive in water? Amphibians such as salamanders and frogs and toads can be used, as I did previously, as an example of this transition.

But what about amphibians? Why do they get to play on both sides of the tracks? Are these creatures simply in the middle of making their evolutionary choice? Are they on their way to the sea or land? We will explore this and similar questions in a later chapter.

Animal evolution has many of the same problems as plant evolution. At the risk of getting repetitive, let us revisit and further explore some of those problems. While exact numbers of species for plants and animals are hard to nail down there are many more animal species than plant. From an evolutionary stand point this makes sense. As we discussed before animal cells evolving before plant cells is the most logical route for the process to have taken. However, as previously discussed the vast variety of species seems to contradict what we would find from an evolutionary process starting with a single cell and working outwards.

While plant varieties are certainly distinctive one from another the difference in the spectrum of animals is much greater than among plants. From tiny sea creatures such as plankton to the giant whales that feed on them. From tiny, imperceptible insects such as dust mites to the titan beetle or the two-foot-long giant walking stick. From a little shrew to a mammoth elephant. From a hummingbird to an albatross. Animal varieties are vast and impressive.

As with plants, we have to ask what are the survival benefits of all these different types of animals? Why dogs and cats? Why birds and flying insects? One could argue there are flying insects so other flying things can eat. How is that evolutionarily acceptable to the insect? We'll talk more about the food chain shortly.

If we look at a specific animal species, it is easy to see how that animal is equipped to successfully handle the environment in which they are found. Survival of the fittest tells us the animals thrive in these environments because of a long period of trial and error. If you look back a few thousand or a couple of million years ago, this same general animal would not be as well adapted for the environment as they are now. Given evolutionary theory, in another couple of million years these animals which seem so well suited to their environments will look quite different and be even more successfully suited to where they are found. This is something we will explore in more depth shortly.

Just as plant scientists breed specific characteristics into or out of vegetation so do animal breeders. Championship horses are prized as biological gold if you want to birth other championship horses. New mixes of dogs are created, seemingly yearly. It seems there have always been a large variety of dogs but now we have created such breeds as the afador, bullmatian, pitt plott, and chiweenie. All of these new breeds take characteristics of the parent species and mix them in inventive, sometimes comical ways.

But they are still dogs, and they still demonstrate many of the aspects of their parents. If you are familiar with the looks of a bull dog and a Dalmatian it is easy to see both of them in the bullmation. Occasionally an article or discussion regarding animals, particularly our domesticated pets, will mention over breeding. In an attempt to bring out the more appealing characteristics of an animal we create health problems within the breed. These man-made, pseudo-evolutionary changes are being found to not be beneficial to the animal. Even with an intelligent attempt to make changes to inhabitants of our world we run into considerable issues. How many more were they to be based solely on chance?

Breeders have also been breeding out unwanted personality traits of certain breeds for hundreds of years. English bull dogs were bred to be nasty, tenacious, dangerous dogs. When the breed was no longer going to be used to fight bulls those traits were not only no longer necessary, but unwanted. Through careful selection of parents these dogs' temperaments were calmed to make them loving, tolerant pets. These new generations were always English bull dogs.

Speaking of breeding, different animal species reproduce in slightly different ways, but one thing that is always the case is a male and female from the species need to work together in order to create offspring. This means in order for a species to pass along its genetic material a male and female would need to evolve compatible parts at the same time. If one gender was a bit late or their parts didn't quite work with the other's that species would die out immediately.

Why is it that, naturally, intercourse between the male and female of the species does not always result in offspring? It seems horribly inefficient to have to keep trying if one wants offspring. This is especially true of human reproduction where the window of conception is quite small. We as humans have developed artificial means to make the process of reproduction even more unlikely. This hardly seems evolutionarily wise.

The question can also be raised to ask why advanced species do not have the ability to reproduce as individuals. Why is it necessary to have two parties to create offspring? The earliest forms of life reproduced individually, when and how was it made necessary for this to change?

Moving back briefly to the topic of animal evolution, I have to ask the question, from what line of animals did the duck billed platypus evolve from? Can it trace its ancestors back to ducks, beavers, penguins, or something else entirely? Just a little food for thought.

Chapter Seven

Then God said, "Let us make man in our image, after our likeness. And let them have dominion over the fish of the sea and over the birds of the heavens and over the livestock and over all the earth and over every creeping thing that creeps on the earth."

-Genesis 1:26.

Where we are going as a species is a big question. Human evolution certainly hasn't stopped. Every time individuals produce a new zygote, there's a reshuffling

*and recombination of genes. And we don't
know where all of that is going to take us.*

-Donald Johanson

*Human evolution, at first, seems
extraordinary. How could the process
that gave rise to slugs and oak trees and
fish produce a creature that can fly to the
moon and invent the Internet and cross
the ocean in boats?*

-Steven Pinker

Let us now turn our attention to humans. Arguably animals, arguably more. Without question, however, we are the dominant species on this planet. We are so dominant in fact, we have to try and hold ourselves in check so we don't completely obliterate all the other species and kill the planet we are living on. Or, in other words, we are on top of the food chain.

Certainly humans are occasionally devoured by wild, and sometimes domesticated animals. This however, is most certainly the exception and not the rule! Before we dig too far into the concept of human evolution, I want to take a little time and look at this food chain. This need for living things to consume energy, feed, and have the need for something to feed on.

Humans, at the top of the chain are omnivorous. We eat plants and animals, with the exception of those who choose to be vegetarians. Our bodies can function on either plant or animal sources of food. In fact, the more variety of food we put into our system the better off we are. Our quality of life decreases the more limited our food options. Humans are not the only omnivores - bears and birds also fit into this category.

Being able to survive on multiple types of food makes sense from an evolutionary point of view. However, there are rather few species which actually adhere to an omnivorous diet. And as I just stated, variety is important in improving quality of life. The greater the quality of life, generally speaking, the longer the life span. An individual creature's life span is one of, if not the most important, factors to determine if that life was evolutionarily successful. A longer life span indicates a better adaptation and a greater chance to advance the creature's genetic material.

The other types of animal diets are herbivorous and carnivorous. Herbivores eat only plants; while carnivores eat only other animals. It should be noted this only applies to an animal in its natural environment. Pet owners who have ever been curious enough to look at the food bag will note much of our pet's food is not meat but often plants of some sort. As there are more herbivorous animals than carnivorous, we will look at them first.

We have discussed the likelihood of animal cells evolving before plant cells given the plant cells' addition of characteristics. Prior to the evolution of plants or at least their cells, animal organisms in whatever their form would have had to obtain their energy from other sources. Once plants made it onto the scene these same organisms would have to evolve a method for extracting nutrients and energy from this new life form. And it would have had to do it at such a rate the animal species could survive and continue to evolve without decimating the plant population to the point it could no longer survive.

Once we get to modern herbivores we see some pretty distinctive differences in how they go about harvesting the nutrients from the plants they eat. Many herbivores such as cows, goats, and horses graze, eating grasses and some grains. There is a difference even amongst grazing animals as some, like horses, have only a one chambered stomach; whereas other grazers, like cows have multiple chambers in order to get the most nutrition out of their food.

Other herbivores eat the fruit of the plant. Still others eat the leaves of trees or plants. Some animals, such as the koala eat only very specific plants. Others such as orangutans eat fruits from a large variety of plants. For those animals with very limited diets their survival depends on the survival of that food source. This raises the question, did the food source come first and the animal adapted to that food? Or did the animal and food source evolve together? Another possibility is if the animal came across the new plant species and adjusted itself to eat it. This new plant would have to be quite prevalent before being discovered in order to survive being the lone food source for an entire species.

Speaking of plant evolution in regards to food, why do these plants not evolve better means to protect themselves from being food? Some plants utilize creatures eating their berries to populate themselves to other areas. But what about those whose leaves, or entire structure are eaten? One would think, as discussed with trees protecting themselves from harvesting, these plants would be better able to defend themselves in order to ensure survival.

We have spoken a couple of times about the idea animal cells must have developed prior to plant cells. When discussing the food supply we run into a bit of an issue with this idea. Without plants, animal cells and ultimately animals, would need to find another source of nutrition. This could be from other animals. We see animals eating other animals all the time. Today there are multiple food sources and opportunity for carnivores to obtain their food.

But was this the case in the ancient world? Were early animals cannibals, eating their own kind? Did more than one animal species evolve together early on with one being dominant and eating the other? This presents a tricky balance for both, and for all species to survive. If the food is gone the dominant animal dies as well. This balance applies to plant eaters as well. Especially with early plants and animals. How fortunate this balance happened to work out as well as it did.

So now that we have discussed some of the lower life on the food chain let us look more specifically at the top. How did humans become top of the food chain? Now that we are on top we can say our intellect, creativity, and ingenuity keep us on top. Our development of traps, weapons, and shelter keep us safe from more powerful animals. Our development of agriculture, animal breeding and domestication keep us fed.

But have humans and our ancestors always been the most intelligent and inventive? If one were to design the perfect human through evolution I would expect a combination of Einstein and Wolverine. Supremely intelligent with built in weapons, orneriness, and the ability to heal remarkably quick. This isn't quite what we see.

Humans are considered to be the most intelligent creature there is. Though we do have some scientists stating dolphins may be giving us a run for our money. But humans are far from the strongest. In fact, creatures in nearly every category of life can kill a human. We have developed artificial ways to defend ourselves, but what happened before that?

Most people have seen the picture depicting human evolution. It starts with a silhouette that looks suspiciously like a modern chimpanzee, goes through five or six stages and ends up with a modern human standing upright and proud. The purpose of this book is not to dive into the evidence behind these stages of human evolution.

Instead we are going to take this diagram, and the ideas behind it at face value and work from there.

What we see as we look at the idea behind human evolution is the creature becoming taller and standing more upright, but becoming thinner and more frail. At some point in this process intelligence began to dominate physical prowess. Even the early human ancestors do not appear to be able to go toe-to-toe physically with many of the dangerous creatures believed to be around at the same time. When looking at an evolutionary generation or two back we see a thick headed, muscular, hairy specimen which appears better suited to survive in nature than the people we are today. Why did they go away? Why were they replaced with a version dependent upon houses and clothing?

The case for a more intelligent creature taking over for a less intelligent one makes sense. But only if other dominating physical characteristics remain. Again one would expected the dominant creature, developed through survival of the fittest to be intelligent but physically imposing and capable of easy survival in nature with and without the tools we have developed. Maybe that man is coming. We'll continue to explore this possibility shortly.

Chapter Eight

There are no shortcuts in evolution.

-Louis D. Brandeis

I encourage people who don't believe in evolution to look for horses in Jurassic Solenhofen limestone.

-Jack Horner

Darwin's theory of evolution is a framework by which we understand the diversity of life on Earth. But there is no equation sitting there in Darwin's 'Origin of Species' that you apply and say, 'What is this species going to look like in 100

years or 1,000 years?' Biology isn't there
yet with that kind of predictive precision.

-Neil deGrasse Tyson

What course does evolution take? The general thought is that it has taken billions of years to get to where we are now through mutations, trial and error, and survival of those best adapted to the environment. We can look at something like, say a hummingbird and describe how its current anatomy allows it to thrive in the environments in which it is found. It is much harder, however, to work backwards to a pre-evolved state and decide just how this new creature came about. The fossil record, to this point, is little help as we simply do not have the evidence of the transition creatures.

Let us use our imaginations and look at a key aspect of the before mentioned hummingbird and see if we can map out the evolution of a hummingbird mouth. A hummingbird has a long beak with an even longer tongue. The hummingbird uses this beak to probe the depths of various flowers allowing it to drink the nectar found inside. The hummingbird's tongue is longer than the beak in order actually make contact with the nectar. This system is an advantage to the hummingbird as it allows it a food source many other birds cannot access.

But what did the hummingbird look like prior to the evolution of this long beak and tongue? Did the humming bird start with a short beak and tongue - similar to most other birds? How quickly did these components grow and change? Which changed first? Did the beak and tongue evolve at exactly the same time? Let's dive more deeply into these questions.

One must assume a hummingbird's mouth started off a good deal smaller than we find it today. Most birds have relatively short beaks while the hummingbird has a comparatively very long beak. If we want to track all birds back to a common ancestor it would make more sense for an initial short mouth. So how quickly did the hummingbird mouth grow? If we say an average hummingbird beak is three-quarters of an inch long and assume, for the sake of argument, ancient hummingbirds had beaks one-quarter of an inch long, how long did it take to develop that additional half-inch? Was the next successful evolution a sixteenth longer? An eighth? A quarter of an inch? Did we get a full half inch jump? And at what point along this evolutionary trail is this bird considered a new species?

Often we hear it asked, "which came first, the chicken or the egg?" In case of the hummingbird we have to ask, "which came first, the beak or the tongue?" Not only do hummingbirds have long beaks but exceedingly long tongues as well. So as the hummingbird evolved did the beak grow first leaving the tongue to play catch up? Did the tongue grow first and then the beak caught up? Can you picture a hummingbird flitting by a flowering plant with a long tongue dangling out of a short beak? The bird flipping its head in order to flick the tongue into the heart of the flower in order to obtain the nectar. Or maybe the tongue stuck out just a little past the beak like a panting dog.

What if the beak evolved longer and longer first? How exactly did the hummingbird get access to the nectar? It is quite possible the variety of food sources would be smaller until the tongue grew longer. But did the bird use the beak to obtain the nectar more like a straw until the tongue caught up? If that was the case, why did the tongue need to grow if the beak was working?

A third option is the two components of the hummingbird's mouth evolved at the same time. Given the randomness and chance centered constructs of evolution this appears to be a stretch. When we look at modern hummingbirds, it is clear the tongue extends well past the beak. If the two pieces evolved at the same time, did they evolve at the same rate? Was the ratio of tongue to beak always the same? How would this have happened by mere chance?

While we are on the subject of the evolution of extended body parts, let us look briefly at the giraffe. We can look at a modern giraffe and state it is successful due to its long neck and legs, which allow it to reach foliage other animals do not have access to. But what about the ancient giraffe? The modern giraffe has very long legs and of course a very long neck. Which of these came first? I would love to see an ancient giraffe with its current incredibly long legs and a short, horse-like neck. Or what about the other way around - an extended neck and stubby legs? And we think the modern giraffe is funny looking!

The giraffe only has seven vertebrae in its neck. These are obviously quite long bones and it is not hard to picture them slowly getting longer in order for the giraffe to reach its current height. But did they keep their current ratios to each other the entire time? Or did one vertebrae get up to its current size before the others started to evolve? Maybe they all started to evolve to be longer but at different rates. Unless all the vertebrae evolved at the same time the order of growth would be critical. If upper vertebrae grew longer, and thus heavier, first they would crush the lower. Yet another piece to this puzzle that had to go just right for this animal to come together.

How did blood get all the way up to its head once it got taller without the heart evolving at the same time? We know giraffes have special valves slowing down blood flow to the brain when it lowers its head to drink. Without these the giraffe would pass out from the high blood pressure and most likely drown instead of drink. When did this come about? Did all three of these systems evolve at the same time, at the same rate? Now we are talking about chances and coincidences melding together in a way almost beyond imagination. The odds of all of this happening at the same time, in order to not kill this evolving animal are beyond comprehension.

The odds of any creature successfully evolving based solely on chance are staggering. Even the phrase astronomical doesn't begin to give a clear picture of everything that must come together to make evolution work.

This super gradual change versus significant leaps does not apply just to animals. As discussed in a previous chapter, the formation of a cell wall and chloroplasts for plants had to take place sometime during the evolutionary process. Did the wall start off as we see it today? Did it begin as a slightly thicker membrane which slowly became more solid? If this is the case, why does a cell membrane remain? Did this wall always completely surround the cell or did it start off smaller and eventually grow to encompass the cell?

We've spent the last few pages working backwards from a life form very well suited to its environment. We have tried to decide what their ancient ancestors may have been like. But looking at these animals and plants which appear to be perfectly at home in their natural environments brings up yet another question. Is evolution finished?

The idea behind evolution is for individuals, and ultimately species, to continue to change and adapt in order to better survive in the environments in which they find themselves. To use unique changes to outlast those without that change. To be somehow superior and find a superior mate to continue on the superiority. But where do we see this as being necessary? How many plants or animals can we come up with for which we say, "man if that thing doesn't change dramatically in the next few thousand years, there is no way it will survive?"

Even the amphibious creatures we spoke of before appear to be at home in their environments. In fact, thriving in two worlds seems like an evolutionary advantage. Either amphibians are still trying to figure out which world they live in, or have a head start on the evolutionary process by being more adaptable. When will other creatures begin to follow suit?

What animals do we see suffering from mass, natural extinction? It is certainly true many animals have gone extinct or are on the verge of extinction, but this has nothing to do with the natural environment and everything to do with humans. The species that dominates the planet. The only species currently equipped to obliterate every other living thing on the planet. In some cases, we have diminished animal populations slowly through hunting and the shrinking of natural habitats. Now when I say slowly I mean that only in a modern sense. In an evolutionary sense we are making changes much faster than a trial and error process could hope to catch up. But we have the ability to take out all life nearly instantly through nuclear weapons.

All this to say, we do not see species of plants or animals decreasing or being eliminated due to poor adaptation to their environment. While we may not expect to see the process of evolution in our comparatively short period of recorded history we should be able to see where evolution is needed. This simply is not the case.

Humans have learned to modify, change, and tinker with various organisms but we have yet to see this need naturally. It is true we see differences within species. If we look back at the hummingbird some have straight beaks while others have curved. There does not seem to be an evolutionary advantage to either one. We cannot predict in a million years if all hummingbirds will have straight or curved beaks. Or maybe the curved beak is on the path of evolution to a curled beak like a kid's twisty straw. Or maybe in a million years there will be hummingbirds with three foot beaks. But why would any of these things occur when the hummingbird flourishes now?

Chapter Nine

All that stuff I was taught about evolution, embryology, the Big Bang theory, all that is lies straight from the pit of Hell. And it's lies to try to keep me and all the folks who were taught that from understanding that they need a savior.

-Paul Broun

All things were made through him, and without him was not anything made that was made.

-John 1:3

For science, the end of the evolution struggle is simply represented by *'survival.' As for the means to that end, apparently anything goes. Darwinism leaves humanity without a moral compass.*

-Bruce Lipton

We have spent a great deal of time looking at all the things that have to come together in order for evolution to be the cause and origin of all there is. It is now time to look at an alternative. Once we flesh out this alternate view we will determine which is the horse and which is the zebra; though I believe it will be quiet obvious by that point if it isn't already.

Many, but not all, religions believe in some sort of creator being. Some of these include Hinduism, Judaism, Christianity, and Islam. This is far from an exhaustive list however it does include most of the world's major religions. For many who are raised in a religious environment the idea behind a creator is a given, little thought is generally put into whether this idea makes any logical sense.

This lack of logical thought by proponents of creationism has left many champions of evolution to see the idea of a Creator as unnecessary at best, foolish wishful thinking by unintelligent morons at worst. There almost seems to be the idea because some who choose to believe in creation have not chosen to develop an argument for it, they are unable to. This is clearly not the case and this chapter seeks to look logically at the basis for a creator.

To some extent the previous chapters went a long way to supporting the evidence of a creator. We saw the vast number of chances and coincidences that are needed in order to make evolution feasible. This does not make evolution impossible, but most definitely improbable. Is a creator being any less probable than the random chances of evolution?

As we look around our world today we see order, structure, and synergy. The natural world around us makes sense. We see squirrels with sharp claws and big bushy tails running up and down trees, jumping from branch to branch, and digging pesky holes in our yards. Do they do this because they discovered by chance they are good at these things? Or are they good at these things because they were designed to be?

There is a substantial organization to the food chain and hierarchy of what eats what. Is this because some being with power and foreknowledge created this or because thousands of species of plants and animals happened to come about and fall into this organization?

The natural world is a jigsaw puzzle with all the pieces fitting together masterfully in order to create a remarkable picture. Did this puzzle come about by chance? Coincidence? An actual puzzle does not come about by chance. It takes several steps to create a jigsaw puzzle. And then even more steps in order to put it together.

There are several analogies used to describe the logic of a Creator for the universe. The previous picture of a jigsaw puzzle for one. Another is a computer. It has been said if you picked someone up from the past and brought them to the future and put them in a room with a computer they would be amazed and wonder who made this machine. They would not automatically assume it randomly came together.

Science had made leaps and bounds to create our modern medicines and technology. These leaps and bounds came about through hard work, planning, and forethought. We have to work hard to create what we have but we assume everything natural just happened to happen. That seems to be a contradictory thought pattern.

If we look just briefly at the laws of thermodynamics we see that left to their own devices things fall apart; they do not come together. Any home owner can attest to this. We have massive stores which are in business for the lone purpose to make money off our houses falling apart. Phrases such as home repair, spring cleaning, and well maintained populate our conversations. We do not have conversations about our self-repairing roofs, our self-organizing closets, or our maintenance-free vehicles.

Why do we ignore this and assume things must be changing for the better? Why do say mutations are good things when all we see from them are cancers and other diseases? Children are told not to stand directly in front of the microwave because of the radiation. Wouldn't we want the radiation? Wouldn't we want the chance to mutate into something else? We'll dive into this a little more in the last chapter.

Comic books make mutations look fascinating, giving those exposed to them super powers. In reality this is not the case. We have yet to run across a beneficial mutation. But what about plain old, ordinary humans? How did our frail, fleshy, nearly hairless bodies ever get the chance to evolve the intelligence needed to become the dominant species on our planet? Evolution should have us being killed off very early in our attempts at survival. Our babies take years before they are even close to being able to protect themselves. Most animals take weeks, or maybe months before they are able to fend for themselves as if they were adults. Humanity's survival and climb to the top in itself is a slap in the face of evolution.

Science tells us matter is neither created nor destroyed, simply changed into different states. This is true except when it comes to how matter came to be in the first place. Evolution can present a theory as to what happened once this matter came into being but it cannot explain where matter came from. A creating being can.

Okay, if a creator created matter, what created the creator? This question is often presented in order to refute the idea of a creator. But who says this creator had to be created? Is it not possible for a supreme being outside of time, space, and matter to exist and choose to create something? Is that not at least as likely as a random occurrence of trillions of small changes ranging over billions of years giving us what we have now? And when I speak of this supreme power being outside of time I mean this being created time along with everything else we know of in our universe. This is not simply a being which happened to phase in from some other dimension.

It is nearly time to make your decision as to which is the horse and which is the zebra.

Evolution cannot give us an answer as to where matter came from. It cannot tell us where the materials spread through the big bang came from. Even the answers evolution gives us after the appearance of matter are hard to comprehend. The astronomical chances required for even the simplest of life forms to come about make evolution illogical. That is not even looking at the amazingly complex biology of humans or the way our world fits together as if designed to do so.

An intelligent, powerful being living outside time, space and matter can account for the appearance of matter from nothing. A creator can explain the fine tuning of the universe in order for life to thrive. A creator can account for the numerous species working together to provide life for each other rather than fighting for superiority and survival. A creator can explain why species of both plants and animals seem to fit into their environments without need for additional adaptations. Only a creator can account for humanity.

Chapter Ten

With evolution, things are always changing, so I sort of think: Should we all be growing three heads?

-Karl Pilkington

If you accept that people are the products of evolution, then you have to have an open mind to the truth. Unfair discrimination exists whether we like it or not; I wouldn't have married a gum-chewing vegetarian.

-James D. Watson

In this chapter I want to explore whether we, in our Western society actually live as if we believe in evolution. Just as those who grow up in a religion that believes in a creator may not question it, those who grow up hearing nothing but evolution may believe it without question. But do they believe it to the point where they act on it? Do we as a society act in a way that demonstrates a sincere belief in evolution?

I want to make one thing very, very clear. It is my opinion that if we lived as if we truly believed in evolution horrible things would be condoned. I will discuss those things in this chapter. What I want to be clear is that I endorse NONE of these things. I do not believe in discrimination against ANYONE for ANY REASON. I believe all human life is sacred. I believe all people should be treated with love, not hate.

If we, in our society truly believed in evolution I think things would be much different. For one thing I think some things considered issues which require medical intervention would be looked at differently. When a baby is born with a sixth finger on a hand it is tied off and let to die and fall off. Wouldn't evolution tell us to celebrate that child? To allow that finger to survive and possibly lead to more people with more fingers? What new pitches could be created with more fingers? Gripping a football to throw or catch would have to be easier with more fingers right?

And what about children born with cleft palates? I understand these children are required to undergo several, often painful procedures in order to repair this condition; but wouldn't evolution tell us to leave it and see where it goes? Couldn't this be the next step in human evolution? As it stands it may present problems with eating and oral health but maybe society should adapt to this new change as opposed to the other way around.

When my youngest son was born he had a minor abnormality. There was no question in the doctor's mind this would need to be corrected in the future. The plan to fix this was stated before the umbilical cord was even cut. There was not even a debate about whether to let the condition continue so as to allow this trait to possibly influence the next evolutionary generation of humans.

As I stated before, in no way do I condone violence or hate towards an individual or group of people, but doesn't evolution tell us some people are inferior? The world was outraged, and rightfully so, when Adolf Hitler determined one race of people was far superior to all others. The world was so outraged a war spanning across the globe broke out. Evolutionarily speaking wasn't Hitler right? If evolution adheres to the survival of the fittest doesn't that mean someone or some group is the fittest? And if one group is the fittest, shouldn't they do whatever is required to ensure their survival?

Our society has embraced homosexuals, their lifestyles, and marriages. Whatever your thoughts on the morality of homosexuality, from a purely evolutionary perspective society should be railing against homosexuality. The continued propagation of homosexuality, taken to its logical conclusion, means the end of the human race as we know it. As our biology stands at this time two men cannot biologically create offspring. Nor can two women. This would mean an increase in homosexuals would lead to a decrease in humans.

The alternative would be for the evolutionary process to change human anatomy in order for two people of the same sex to biologically create offspring. This would be a new species which inevitably would compete with humans, as we now stand, for superiority.

What of children with severe birth defects? We as a society spend billions of dollars on equipment, time, and care for these children. We spend billions on the elderly as well. Evolution tells us these people are of no value and our resources are wasted taking care of them. Remember, survival of the fittest. If you need that much help to survive are you anywhere near the fittest?

Evolution paints a dark picture; it creates a dark path for society to follow. If we treated people the way evolution dictates, this would not be a world worth living in. If we condoned the actions of those who believe they are superior and have a right to demonstrate that, our world would be frightening. If we did not treat those less fortunate with love and compassion, our world would be cold.

Our society may speak of evolution, we may teach it in our schools, and we may feel those who disagree with the "law of evolution" are ignorant, but thank God we do not act on this supposed belief in evolution. Thank God we use compassion and understanding. Thank God we see value in life for life's sake and not because it can help us up another rung of the evolutionary ladder.

Chapter Eleven

For his invisible attributes, namely, his eternal power and divine nature, have been clearly perceived, ever since the creation of the world, in the things that have been made. So they are without excuse.

-Romans 1:20

You can't even begin to understand biology, you can't understand life, unless you understand what it's all there for, how it arose - and that means evolution.

-Richard Dawkins

After looking at both evolution and creationism in a straight-forward, good sense, logical way what conclusions can we come to? Which theory is the horse and which is the zebra?

One thing is for certain, despite what many proponents of both sides may say, both theories require a level of faith. One can choose to put faith in a seemingly endless string of random occurrences - occurrences which take you from absolute nothingness to our vast array of plant and animal life, organized in a way in which nearly everything can survive and thrive on a planet that is properly placed to be conducive to these things.

Or, one could choose faith in a supreme being that exists outside of time, space, and matter that has the power, creativity, and desire to create a complex system of life and nature which makes everything stable. A Creator who designed the puzzle pieces to fit perfectly in order to show the picture conceived since the beginning of time.

Just as we looked at the animal in London, applying those same principles allows us to better focus on the reality of these two theories. Are both theories possible? I am hard pressed to grant evolution a place at the possible table given the near impossibility of the number of coincidences which would have had to happen for the theory to work. But for the sake of argument, we will give evolution a pass into the possible realm. Is it possible for the existence of a supreme being with the power to create? I believe it is.

Do both theories completely answer the question of the beginning of the universe and life as we know it? I believe evolution has too many questions which are unanswered. I think the biggest one is the introduction of matter into and from nothingness. Does a creator completely answer our question? Yes.

At this point, given evolution's inability to fully answer our question we can be finished with our logical assessment. But for the sake of thoroughness let us look at which answer is the simplest. By far that is the idea of a creator bringing everything we know into existence.

In my opinion evolution not only leaves many more holes than creation - it requires much more faith and has almost no hope of explaining where matter originated. Evolution also lends itself to a cold, dangerous, hateful world. Each person is free to draw their own conclusion as to which theory is worth putting their faith in. I think it is clear evolution is nothing more than the apparition of a zebra when there is a horse right in front of us.

References

1.Cell Biology, Structure, Biochemistry, and Function 2nd edition. Phillip Sheeler & Donald Bianchi. New York. 1983.

2.The World of the Cell: Life on a Small Scale. Robert Snedden. Chicago. 2003.

3.Giantgardening.com/rec_tomato.php